Mikhail GORBACHEV

October and Perestroika: the Revolution Continues

Report by the General Secretary of the CPSU Central Committee at the jubilee meeting of the Central Committee of the CPSU, the Supreme Soviet of the USSR and the Supreme Soviet of the RSFSR to mark the 70th anniversary of the Great October Socialist Revolution

November 2, 1987

Novosti Press Agency
Publishing House
Moscow 1987

Reprinted by: Press Office of the USSR Embassy
OTTAWA 1987

0902040000

© Novosti Press Agency Publishing House, 1987

Reprinted by: Press Office of the USSR Embassy
OTTAWA 1987

Dear Comrades,
Esteemed foreign guests,

It is seventy years since the unforgettable days of October 1917, those legendary days that started the count of the new epoch of social progress, of the real history of mankind. The October Revolution is truly humanity's finest hour, its radiant dawn. The October Revolution is a revolution of the people and for the people, for every individual, for his emancipation and development.

Seventy years is nothing compared to world civilisation's ascent through the centuries, but in terms of the scale of achievements history has known no other period like the one our country has experienced since the victory of the October Revolution. There is no greater honour than to be pioneers, devoting one's strength, energy, knowledge, and ability to the triumph of the October Revolution's ideas and goals!

The jubilee is an occasion for pride. Pride in what has been achieved. Severe trials fell to our lot. And we withstood them honourably. We did not simply withstand them, but wrested the country out of its state of dislocation and backwardness, turned it into a mighty power, transformed life and changed man's inner world beyond recognition.

In the cruelest battles of the 20th century we safeguarded the right to our own way of life, and defended our future. We have legitimate grounds for pride in the fact that our Revolution, our labour and struggle continue to exercise a most profound influence on all aspects of world development—politics and the economy, the social sphere, and the consciousness of our contemporaries.

The jubilee is an occasion for remembrance. To remember those millions of people who have each contributed to our common socialist gains. To remember those who smelted steel, grew crops, taught children, developed science and technology, and attained the summits of art. And in sad memory of those who fell in battle defending the country, and enabled our society to advance at the price of their lives. In unfading recollection of what we have lived through, of the path we have travelled, because it was all this that created the present day.

The jubilee is an occasion for reflection. On how difficult and complicated our affairs and destinies were at times. There were not only heroic feats but tragedies, not only great victories but bitter failures as well. We reflect on the seventy years of intense constructive endeavour from the positions of the people ready to mobilise all their strength and socialism's enormous potential for the revolutionary transformation of life.

The jubilee is also a glance into the future. Our achievements are imposing, substantial and significant. They are a lasting foundation, the basis for new attainments and for society's further development. It is in advancing socialism and in developing the ideas and practices of Leninism and the October Revolution that we see the substance of our present-day affairs and concerns, our prime task and moral duty. And that necessitates serious and thorough analysis of the historical significance of the October Revolution, of everything that has been done in these seventy post-October years.

I. The October Road: Road of Trailblazers

Comrades, our road as trailblazers has been long and difficult. No brief analysis can encompass it. There was the burden of the material and moral heritage left over by the old world, World War I, the Civil War, and the intervention. There was the novelty of change and the related hopes of people, the rate and scale of the invasion of the new and unusual, sometimes leaving us no time to look around and think. There were subjective factors, which play a special part in the periods of revolutionary storms. There were notions of the future, often simplistic and straightforward, and full of the maximalism of revolutionary times. And there were also the pure, ardent strivings of the fighters for a new life to accomplish things as quickly, as well, and as fairly as possible.

The past—its heroism and drama—cannot fail to thrill our contemporaries. We have one history, and it is irreversible. Whatever emotions it may evoke, it is our history, and we cherish it. Today we turn to those October days that shook the world. We look for and find in them both a dependable spiritual support, and instructive lessons. We see once again that the socialist option of the October Revolution has been correct.

The objective logic of mankind's historical progress had led up to that frontier. For all the contradictions and the many possible ways of civilisation's progressive development, the October Revolution was a natural result of the development of the ideas and the many centuries of the working people's struggle for freedom and peace, for social justice, and against class, national, and spiritual oppression.

The year 1917 showed that the choice between socialism and capitalism is the main social alternative of our epoch, that in the 20th century there can be no progress without advance to socialism, a higher form of social organisation. This fundamental conclusion is no less relevant today than when it was first drawn by Lenin. Such is the logic of society's progressive development.

The Revolution in Russia has become, as it were, the summit of the aspirations for liberation, the living embodiment of the dreams of the world's finest minds—from the great humanists of the past to the proletarian revolutionaries of the 19th and 20th centuries. The year 1917 absorbed the energy of the people's struggle for self-sustained development and independence, of the progressive national movements, and the peasant uprisings and wars against serfdom abounding in our history. It embodied the spiritual search of the 18th-century enlighteners, the heroes and martyrs of the Decembrist movement, and the ardent champions of revolutionary democracy, and the moral dedication of the prominent figures in our culture.

Crucial for the future of our country was the time when at the dawn of the 20th century Vladimir Ilyich Lenin put himself at the head of a close-knit group of like-minded people and set out to organise a proletarian party of a new type in Russia. It was this great Party of Lenin that roused the nation, its best and most devoted forces, for an assault on the old world.

The cornerstone in the success of the October Revolution was laid by the First Russian Revolution of 1905-1907. This includes the bitter lessons of the Ninth of January, the desperate heroism of people fighting on the Moscow barricades in December, the exploit of thousands of known and unknown freedom fighters, and the birth of the first workers' Soviets, the prototypes of Soviet power.

The victory of the October Revolution was also rooted in the gains of the February 1917 Revolution, the first victorious people's revolution in the imperialist epoch. After the February victory the Revolution went forward with incredible speed. Its leading characters were the workers and peasants wearing soldiers' greatcoats. The spring of 1917 showed all the might of the people's movement. At the same time, there surfaced its limitations, the contradictions in the revolutionary consciousness at that stage, the power of historical inertia, with the result that for a time the exploiter classes departing from the scene took advantage of the fruits of the people's victory.

The February Revolution provided the October Revolution with its main weapon—power organised in the revived Soviets. The February Revolution had been the first experience of real democracy, of political education of the masses through an experience acquired in the intricate conditions of dual power. The February Revolution was unique in that it provided an opportunity for power to be taken over peacefully by the working people—something which, regrettably, did not finally come about owing to historical circumstances. The February Revolution was a major historical landmark on the road to the October Revolution.

In the complicated intertwining and confrontation of the class forces that were involved in the February Revolution, Lenin, with the insight of genius, saw opportunities for the victory of a socialist revolution. His April Theses were a scientific foresight and a model of a revolutionary action programme in those historical conditions. Lenin made clear not only the logic of the bourgeois-democratic revolution growing over into a socialist revolution, but also the form of that process—through the Soviets, through their Bolshevisation, the essence of which was to help the people, the masses, to understand the purpose of their own struggle, and to carry out the revolution consciously in their own interests. The road from the February to the October Revolution was a time of swift social change, a time of a rapid growth of the political awareness of the masses, of a consolidation of the revolutionary forces and their vanguard, the Party of Lenin.

At that time, between February and October, Lenin and his comrades-in-arms demonstrated the art of political guidance with extraordinary force, supplying a good lesson in the living dialectics of revolutionary thought and action. The Party leadership showed its ability for collective creative search, getting rid of stereotypes and slogans that had only yesterday, in a different situation, seemed incontestable and the only possibility. One may say that the very course of Lenin's thought, the entire activity of the Bolsheviks, marked by swift change of form and method, flexibility, unusual tactical solutions, and by political audacity—all this was a vivid example of anti-dogmatic, truly dialectical, and therefore new, way of thinking. That and only that is how real Marxist-Leninists think and act—especially at times of change, at critical turning points, when the future of the revolution and peace, socialism and progress, is at stake.

Let us go back to April 1917: to many, both friends and foes, Lenin's programme of going over to a socialist revolution seemed a utopia, something next to unbridled fantasy. But life has shown that only such a programme could and did become the political foundation for the further development of the revolution and, in fact, the basis for social salvation, for averting national catastrophe.

Let us recall the July days of 1917. It was a painful moment when the Party was compelled to give up the slogan of passing power to the Soviets. But there was no other choice, because the Soviets had, for a while, fallen into the hands of Socialist-Revolutionaries and Mensheviks, and were helpless before the counter-revolution. And how sensitive Lenin was to the pulse of the Revolution, how brilliantly he determined the beginning of a new revival of the Soviets, which, in the process of struggle, were acquiring a truly popular essence, which enabled them to become the organs of a victorious armed uprising, and then also the political form of worker-peasant government.

All this is not simply pages in the chronicle of the Great Revolution. This is also a constant reminder to us, those who are living today, of the lofty duty of Communists always to be in the vanguard of events, to be able to take bold decisions, to assume full responsibility for the present and future.

The October Revolution was a powerful surge of millions of people which combined the vital interests of the working class, the everlasting aspirations of the peasantry, the thirst for peace of soldiers and sailors, and the unconquerable striving of the peoples of multinational Russia for freedom and enlightenment. The Bolshevik Party managed to find the main point in that intricate conglomerate of diverse interests, to combine the different tendencies and aspirations, and to concentrate them on solving the Revolution's main issue, that of power. And in its very first decrees, those on peace and on land, the state of the dictatorship of the proletariat responded to the needs of the time, and expressed the vital interests of the working class and, indeed, the absolute majority of the people.

Today, it is essential that we remember one more important, fundamental lesson of those October days. Highly relevant in our time is Lenin's reply to the question posed by life, by revolutionary activity—the question about the relationship of the theoretical "model" of the road to socialism and the actual practices of socialist construction. Marxism-Leninism is a creative doctrine, not a set of ready-made guidelines and doctrinaire prescriptions. Foreign to all sorts of dogmatism, the Marxist-Leninist doctrine ensures vigorous interaction between innovative theoretical thought and practice, the very course of the revolutionary struggle. The October Revolution is a most instructive example thereof.

It will be recalled that many leaders of the working-class movement of those days, even prominent ones, did not see the October Socialist Revolution as an objective development: they held that it went against the "rules", that it was contrary to the prevailing theoretical views. As they saw it, capitalism in Russia had not created all the requisite material and cultural preconditions for socialism by October 1917. It is instructive and useful, I think, to recall what Lenin replied to these critics of our Revolution. "You say that civilisation is necessary for the building of socialism," he retorted. "Very good. But why could we not first create such prerequisites of civilisation in our country as the expulsion of the landowners and the Russian capitalists, and then start moving towards socialism?"

Those who treat Marxism dogmatically and pedantically cannot understand its central point: its revolutionary dialectic. This latter is characteristic of all of Lenin's post-revolution activity. It helped accomplish the political and moral exploit of the Brest Peace literally on the edge between the possible and impossible, saving thousands upon thousands of lives and securing the very survival of the socialist Motherland.

One more example. Like Marx and Engels, Lenin was convinced that the armed defence of the Revolution would be provided by a people's militia. But the concrete conditions prompted a different solution. The Civil War and the intervention from outside, imposed on the people, called for a new approach. A worker-peasant Red Army was formed by Lenin's decree. It was an army of a new type which covered itself with eternal glory in the Civil War and in repulsing the foreign intervention.

Those years brought severe trials for the newly-established Soviet government. It had to settle the elementary and crucial question of whether socialism would or would not be. The Party mobilised the people to defend the socialist Motherland, the gains of the October Revolution. Hungry, ill-clad and unshod, the poorly armed Red Army crushed a well-trained and well-armed counter-revolutionary army which was being generously supplied by imperialists of East and West. The fiery dividing line of the Civil War ran right across the country, across every family, wreaking havoc with the habitual way of life, with the psychology and fate of people. The will of the nation, the striving of millions towards a new life, won out in this deadly clash. The country did everything it could to help the newly-established army; it lived and acted by Lenin's slogan: "Everything for victory".

We will never forget the exploit of those legendary heroes—gallant sailors and cavalrymen, men and commanders of the young Red Army, and the Red partisans. They had safeguarded the Revolution; everlasting glory is their due!

The decision to launch a new economic policy, which substantially widened the notions of socialism and the ways of building it, was imbued with profound revolutionary dialectics.

Or take the following issue: as you know, Lenin criticised the limitations of "cooperative socialism". Yet in the specific conditions that arose after the October Revolution, when power was won by the people, Lenin had second thoughts on this score. In his article, *On Cooperation*, he put forward the idea of socialism being a society of "civilised cooperators".

Such was the power and audacity of Marxist dialectics, which expressed the essence of the revolutionary doctrine and which Lenin had so brilliantly mastered. He held that in building the new world, we shall have again and again "to improve the work, redo it, start from the beginning".

Yes, we have had to improve and redo things again and again, endure long and hard struggle, and go through historical processes of a crucial, revolutionary nature. And they have in many ways changed the circumstances and conditions of our advance. They also changed us—they seasoned us, enriched us with experience and knowledge, and gave us still greater faith in the success of the Revolution.

Assessing the path we have travelled from the point of view of world history, one sees again and again that we have accomplished in a short time what took others centuries to accomplish.

The socialist revolution occurred in a country with a medium-level development of capitalism, a highly concentrated industry, a predominantly peasant population, and deep-going survivals of feudalism and even of earlier social systems. Russia gave the world truly great achievements in science and culture, even though three-quarters of its population could neither read nor write. The country was ravaged to the extreme by imperialist World War I and an incompetent government.

There were no models to go by in the building of a new life and a tireless search for constructive solutions was required. To the Communist Party the aim was clear: revolution and the socialist path, Soviet government. And Lenin led the Party along that path.

Out of the complex material of multistructured Russia, the principles and standards of the future socialist system crystallised, and so did unprecedented forms of organising society. What in the beginning were purely theoretical notions about the forms of government by the people, about the ways and limits of socialising property, about the organisation of socialist production, the initiation of a new, comradely discipline, and about the place and role of the individual in the new society, were clarified and filled with a real and tangible content.

The main purpose of the October Revolution was to build a new life. And this building did not cease for a single day. Even a short respite was used to continue building and to look for ways leading to the socialist future.

The early 1920s were highlighted by a spectacular surge of popular initiative and creativity. Those years were a truly revolutionary laboratory of social innovation, of a search for the optimal forms of the alliance between the working class and the working peasantry, and of the shaping of a mechanism for meeting all of the working people's interests.

The Party switched over from organising production and consumption by methods of war communism, which had been necessary due to war and dislocation, to more flexible, economically justified, "regular" instruments of influencing social realities. The measures of the new economic policy were directed towards building the material foundations of socialism.

These days we turn ever more often to Lenin's last works, to his ideas of the new economic policy, and seek to extract from this experience everything valuable and needed today. Certainly, it would be a mistake to equate the new economic policy with what we are doing today at a fundamentally new level of development. Today, the country does not have those individual peasants with whom the shaping of an alliance determined the most vital aims of the economic policy of the 1920s.

But the new economic policy also had a more distant target. The task was set of building a new society "not directly relying on enthusiasm," as Lenin wrote, "but aided by the enthusiasm engendered by the great revolution, and on the basis of personal interest, personal incentive and business principles. ... That is what experience, the objective course of the development of the revolution, has taught us."

Speaking of the creative potential of the new economic policy, we should evidently refer once more to the wealth of political and methodological ideas underlying the food tax. We are of course interested not in its forms of those days that had been meant to secure a bond between workers and peasants, but in the potentialities of the idea of the food tax in releasing the creative energy of the masses, enhancing the initiative of the individual, and removing the bureaucratic obstacles that limited the operation of the basic principle of socialism: "From each according to his ability, to each according to his work."

The socialist construction that was started under Lenin's leadership brought about many fundamentally new elements.

Methods of planned economy were worked out and applied for the first time in world history. The General Plan for the Electrification of Russia was indeed a discovery, a whole line of advance in the world's economic thinking and practice. It was not only an imposing electrification plan, but also a project, as conceived by Lenin, of a "harmonious coordination" of agriculture, industry and transport, or, in modern-day terms, a comprehensive programme for the distribution and development of the country's productive forces. Lenin called it the second programme of the Party, "a plan of work aimed at restoring our entire economy and raising it to the level of up-to-date technical development".

A new culture was taking shape, absorbing both past experience and the multicoloured wealth, daring, and originality of talents, of striking personalities whom the Revolution had aroused and inspired to serve the people. Of everlasting significance for us, not only for its results but also for its experience and method, is the initial, Leninist stage of forming the multinational Soviet state.

When thinking of the time when "NEP Russia will become socialist Russia", Lenin could not, and never meant to, draw the picture of the future society in every detail. But the ways and means of advancing to socialism through the building of a machine industry, through a broad-scale establishment of cooperatives, through the enlistment of the working masses to a man in running the state, through organising the work of the state apparatus on the principle of "better fewer, but better" and through the cultural development of the entire mass of the people, through the consolidation of the federation of free nations "without lies or bayonets"—this and this alone was to shape the face of the country as it attained a fundamentally new level of social order.

In Lenin's last works, which were extraordinarily rich intellectually and emotionally, there emerged a system of views and the very concept of socialist construction in our country. This is an immense theoretical asset for the Party.

Lenin's premature death was a terrible shock for the whole Party and the Soviet people. The grief was immeasurable, the loss irreparable. This was clear to everyone. Undertakings of colossal historical importance lay ahead. Without Lenin, relying on his doctrine and his behests, the Party leadership was to find the optimal solutions that could consolidate the gains of the Revolution and lead the country to socialism in the concrete conditions of the Soviet Russia of that time.

History set the new system a rigid ultimatum: either it would in the shortest possible time build its own social, economic and technical basis and survive, giving the world the first example of a just society, or fade out and remain in the memory of time at best as a heroic but unsuccessful social experiment. Vital and crucial significance, in the full sense of the word, was attached to the question of securing a swift rate of socialist change.

The period after Lenin, that is, the 1920s and the 1930s, occupied a special place in the history of the Soviet state. Radical social changes were carried out in about fifteen years. An incredible lot happened in that period—both from the point of view of search for optimal variants of socialist construction, and from the point of view of what was really achieved in building the foundations of the new society. Those were years of hard work to the limits of human endurance, of sharp and multifarious struggle. Industrialisation, collectivisation, the cultural revolution, the strengthening of the multinational state, the consolidation of the Soviet Union's international positions, new forms of managing the economy and all social affairs—all this occurred in that period. And all of it had far-reaching consequences.

For decades, we have been returning to that time again and again. This is natural. Because that was when the world's first socialist society had its beginnings, when it was being built. It was an exploit on a historical scale and of historic significance. Admiration for the exploits of our fathers and grandfathers, and the assessments of our real achievements will live forever, as will the exploits and achievements themselves. And if, at times, we scrutinise our history with a critical eye, we do so only because we want to have a better and fuller idea of the ways that lead to the future.

It is essential to assess the past with a sense of historical responsibility and on the basis of the historical truth. This must be done, firstly, because of the tremendous importance of those years for the future of our country, the future of socialism. Secondly, because those years are in the centre of the everlasting discussions both in our country and abroad, where, along with a search for the truth, attempts are often being made to discredit socialism as a new social system, as a realistic alternative to capitalism. Lastly, we need truthful assessments of this and all the other periods of our history—especially now with the restructuring in full swing. We need them not to settle political scores or, as they say, to let off steam, but to pay due credit to all the heroic things in the past, and to draw lessons from mistakes and miscalculations.

And so, about the 1920s and the 1930s after Lenin. Although the Party and society had Lenin's conception of building socialism and Lenin's works of the post-revolution period to go by, the search for the way was not at all simple; it was marked by keen ideological struggle and political discussions. In their centre were the basic problems of society's development, and above all the question of whether socialism could be built in our country. Theoretical thought and practice were searching for the directions and forms in which to carry out socio-economic transformations, and for the ways to accomplish them on socialist principles in the concrete historical conditions the Soviet Union was in.

Practical constructive work that called for a great sense of responsibility was on the agenda. Above all, the country squarely faced the question of industrialisation and economic reconstruction without which the building of socialism and the strengthening of the defence capability were unthinkable. This followed from Lenin's explicit directions, from his theoretical heritage. The question of socialist changes in the countryside, too, arose on the same plane and also according to Lenin's behests.

Thus, what was involved was large-scale and

crucial matters, problems, and objectives. And though, I repeat, the Party had Lenin's guidelines on these issues, sharp debates started over them.

It is evidently worthwhile to say that before and after the Revolution, in the first few years of socialist construction, far from all Party leaders shared Lenin's views on some of the most important problems. Besides, Lenin's recommendations could not encompass all the concrete issues concerning the building of the new society. Analysing the ideological disputes of those times, we should bear in mind that carrying out gigantic revolutionary transformations in a country such as Russia was then, was in itself a most difficult task. Historically, the country was on the march, its development was being sharply accelerated, and all aspects of social life were changing rapidly and profoundly.

Reflecting the whole range of the interests of classes, social groups and strata, the needs and objectives of the times, the historical traditions and the pressure of urgent tasks, and also the conditions of the hostile capitalist encirclement, the ideological struggle was indissolubly intertwined with events and processes in the economy and politics, and in all spheres of life.

In brief, it was extremely difficult to get one's bearings and find the only correct course in that intricate and stormy situation. To a considerable extent, too, the character of the ideological struggle was complicated by personal rivalries in the Party leadership. The old differences that had existed in Lenin's lifetime, also made themselves felt in the new situation, and this in a very acute form. Lenin, as we know, had warned against this danger. In his *Letter to the Congress* he had stressed that "it is not a detail, or it is a detail which can assume decisive importance". And that was largely what had happened.

Their petty-bourgeois nature took the upper hand in the case of some respectable leaders. They took a factional stance. This agitated the Party organisations, distracted them from vital affairs, and interfered in their work. The leaders in question continued to provoke a split even after the vast majority in the Party saw that their views were contrary to Lenin's ideas and plans, and that their proposals were erroneous and could push the country off the correct course.

This applies first of all to Leon Trotsky, who had, after Lenin's death, displayed excessive pretensions to top leadership in the Party, thus fully confirming Lenin's opinion of him as an excessively self-assured politician who always vacillated and cheated. Trotsky and the Trotskyites negated the possibility of building socialism in conditions of capitalist encirclement. In foreign policy they put their stakes on the export of the revolution, and in home policy on the tightening of the screws on the peasants, on the city exploiting the countryside, and on administrative and military methods in running society. Trotskyism was a political trend whose ideologists took cover behind leftist pseudo-revolutionary rhetoric, and who in effect assumed a defeatist posture. This was actually an attack on Leninism all down the line. The matter practically concerned the future of socialism in our country, the fate of the Revolution.

In these circumstances, it was essential to disprove Trotskyism before the whole people, and expose its anti-socialist essence. The situation was complicated by the fact that the Trotskyites were acting in common with the "new opposition" headed by Grigori Zinoviev and Lev Kamenev. Being aware that they constituted a minority, the opposition leaders had again and again saddled the Party with discussions, counting on a split in its ranks. But in the final analysis, the Party spoke out for the line of the Central Committee and against the opposition, which was soon ideologically and organisationally crushed.

In short, the Party's leading nucleus headed by Joseph Stalin had safeguarded Leninism in an ideological struggle. It defined the strategy and tactics in the initial stage of socialist construction, with its political course being approved by most members of the Party and most working people. An important part in defeating Trotskyism ideologically was played by

Nikolai Bukharin, Felix Dzerzhinsky, Sergei Kirov, Grigori Ordjonikidze, Jan Rudzutak, and others.

At the very end of the 1920s a sharp struggle started over the ways of putting the peasantry on the socialist road. In substance, it revealed the different attitude of the majority in the Political Bureau and of the Bukharin group on how to apply the principles of the new economic policy at the new stage in the development of Soviet society.

The concrete conditions of that time—both at home and internationally—necessitated a considerable increase in the rate of socialist construction. Bukharin and his followers had, in their calculations and theoretical propositions, underrated the practical significance of the time factor in building socialism in the 1930s. In many ways, their posture was based on dogmatic thinking and a non-dialectical assessment of the concrete situation. Bukharin himself and his followers soon admitted their mistakes.

In this connection, it is appropriate to recall Lenin's opinion of Bukharin. "Bukharin," he said, "is not only a most valuable and major theorist of the Party; he is also rightly considered the favourite of the whole Party, but his theoretical views can be classified as fully Marxist only with great reserve, for there is something scholastic about him (he has never made a study of dialectics, and, I think, never fully understood it)." The facts again confirmed that Lenin had been right.

Thus, the political discussions of that time reflected a complex process in the Party's development, marked by acute struggle over crucial problems of socialist construction. In that struggle, which had to be endured, the concept of industrialisation and collectivisation took shape.

Under the leadership of the Party, of its Central Committee, a heavy industry, including engineering, a defence industry and a chemical industry abreast of the times, were built in a brief period practically from scratch, and the General Electrification Plan was completed. These achievements were symbolised by the Magnitogorsk steelmaking plant, the Kuznetsk coalfields, the Dnieper hydropower station, the Ural heavy engineering works, the Khibiny plant, the motor works in Moscow and Gorky, aircraft plants, the Stalingrad, Chelyabinsk and Kharkov tractor works, the Rostov agricultural machinery works, the city of Komsomolsk-on-Amur, the Turksib railway, the Grand Ferghana canal, and many other great building projects of our early five-year plans. Dozens of research institutes and a broad network of higher educational establishments were founded in those days.

The Party charted a previously unknown method of industrialisation: to begin building a heavy industry at once, without reliance on external sources of finance, and without waiting years for capital to accumulate through the expansion of light industry. This was the only possible way in those conditions, though it was incredibly difficult for the country and the people. It was an innovative step in which the revolutionary enthusiasm of the masses was taken into account as a component of economic growth. Industrialisation raised the country to a fundamentally new level in one jump. By the end of the 1930s the Soviet Union had moved to first place in Europe and second place in the world for industrial output, becoming a truly great industrial power. This was a labour exploit of epoch-making significance, an exploit of liberated labour, an exploit of the Bolshevik Party.

And looking at history with a sober eye, considering the aggregate of internal and international realities, one cannot help asking whether a course other than that the Party chose could have been taken in those conditions. If we wish to be faithful to history and the truth of life, there can be only one answer: no other course could have been taken. In those conditions, with the threat of imperialist aggression building up visibly, the Party was increasingly convinced that it was essential not to just cover but literally race across the distance from the sledgehammer and wooden plough to an advanced industry in the shortest possible time, for without this the cause of the Revolution would be inevitably destroyed.

The viability of the Party's plans, understood and accepted by the masses, and of the slogans and objectives embodying the revolutionary spirit of the October Revolution, found expression in the astonishing enthusiasm shown by millions of Soviet people who joined in building the country's industry. In most difficult conditions, in the absence of mechanisation, on semi-starvation rations, people performed miracles. They were inspired by the fact that they had a hand in a great historical cause. Though they were not sufficiently literate, their class instinct told them that they were participating in a momentous and unprecedented undertaking.

It is our duty and the duty of those who will follow us to remember this exploit of our fathers and grandfathers. Everyone must know that their labour and their selfless dedication were not in vain. They coped with everything that fell to their lot, and made a great contribution to the consolidation of the gains of the October Revolution, to laying the foundations of the strength that enabled them to save the Motherland from a deadly peril, to save socialism for the future, for all of us, comrades. Hallowed be their memory!

At the same time, the period under review also saw some losses. They were in a sense connected with the successes I have just referred to. Some had begun to believe in the universal effectiveness of rigid centralisation, in that methods of command were the shortest and best way of resolving any and all problems. This had an effect on the attitude towards people, towards their conditions of life.

A system of administrative command in Party and government leadership emerged in the country, and bureaucratism gained strength, even though Lenin had warned about its danger. And a corresponding structure of administration and methods of planning began to take shape. In industry—given its scale at the time, when literally all the main components of the industrial edifice were conspicuous—such methods, such a system of administration generally produced results. However, an equally rigid centralisation-and-command system was impermissible in tackling the problems of refashioning rural life.

It must be said frankly: at the new stage there was a deficit of the Leninist considerate attitude to the interests of the working peasantry. Most important of all, there was an underestimation of the fact that the peasantry as a class had changed radically in the years since the Revolution. The principal figure now was the middle peasant. He had asserted himself as a farmer working the land he had received from the Revolution and he had, over a whole decade, become convinced that Soviet government was his kind of government. He had become a staunch and dependable ally of the working class—an ally on a new basis, an ally who was becoming convinced from his own experience that his life was increasingly taking a turn for the better.

And if there had been more consideration for objective economic laws and if more attention had been given to the social processes taking place in the countryside, if in general the attitude to this vast mass of the working peasantry, most of whom had taken part in the Revolution and had defended it from the White Guards and the forces of intervention, had been politically more judicious, if there had been a consistent line to promote the alliance with the middle peasant against the kulak, then there would not have been all those excesses that occurred in carrying out collectivisation.

Today it is clear: in a tremendous undertaking, which affected the fate of the majority of the country's population, there was a departure from Lenin's policy towards the peasantry. This most important and very complex social process, in which a great deal depended on local conditions, was directed mostly by administrative methods. A conviction had arisen that all problems could be solved in a stroke, overnight. Whole regions and parts of the country began to compete: which of them would achieve complete collectivisation more quickly. Arbitrary percentage targets were issued from above. Flagrant violations of the principles of collectivisation occurred everywhere. Nor were excesses avoided in the struggle against the kulaks. The basically correct policy of fighting the kulaks was often interpreted so broadly that it swept in a considerable part of the middle peasantry too. Such is the reality of history.

But, comrades, if we assess the significance of collectivisation as a whole in consolidating socialism in the countryside, it was in the final analysis a transformation of fundamental importance. Collectivisation implied a radical change in the entire mode of life of the preponderant part of the country's population to a socialist footing. It created the social base for modernising the agrarian sector and regearing it along the lines of advanced farming techniques; it made possible a considerable rise in the productivity of labour, and it released a substantial share of manpower needed for other spheres of socialist construction. All this had historical effects.

To understand the situation of those years it must be borne in mind that the administrative-command system, which had begun to take shape in the process of industrialisation and which had received a fresh impetus during collectivisation, had told on the whole socio-political life of the country. Once established in the economy, it had spread to its superstructure, restricting the development of the democratic potential of socialism and holding back the progress of socialist democracy.

But the aforesaid does not give a full picture of how complex that period was. What had happened? The time of ideological-political tests of the utmost gravity to the Party was actually over. Millions of people had joined enthusiastically in the work of bringing about socialist transformations. The first successes were becoming apparent. Yet at that time methods dictated by the period of struggle against the hostile resistance of the exploiter classes were being mechanically transferred to the period of peaceful socialist construction, when conditions had changed cardinally. An atmosphere of intolerance, hostility, and suspicion was created in the country. As time went on, this political practice gained in scale, and was backed up by the erroneous "theory" of an aggravation of the class struggle in the course of socialist construction.

All this had a dire effect on the country's socio-political development and produced grim consequences. Quite obviously, it was the absence of a proper level of democratisation in Soviet society that made possible the personality cult, the violations of legality, the wanton repressive measures of the thirties. Putting things bluntly—those were real crimes stemming from an abuse of power. Many thousands of people inside and outside the Party were subjected to wholesale repression. Such, comrades, is the bitter truth. Serious damage was done to the cause of socialism and to the authority of the Party. And we must state this bluntly. This is necessary to assert Lenin's ideal of socialism once and for all.

There is now much discussion about the role of Stalin in our history. His was an extremely contradictory personality. To remain faithful to historical truth we must see both Stalin's incontestable contribution to the struggle for socialism, to the defence of its gains, and the gross political errors, and the abuses committed by him and by those around him, for which our people paid a heavy price and which had grave consequences for the life of our society. It is sometimes said that Stalin did not know about instances of lawlessness. Documents at our disposal show that this is not so. The guilt of Stalin and his immediate entourage before the Party and the people for the wholesale repressive measures and acts of lawlessness is enormous and unforgivable. This is a lesson for all generations.

Contrary to the assertions of our ideological opponents, the personality cult was certainly not inevitable. It was alien to the nature of socialism, represented a departure from its fundamental principles, and, therefore, has no justification. At its 20th and 22nd Congresses the Party severely condemned the Stalin cult itself and its consequences. We now know that the political accusations and repressive measures against a number of Party leaders and statesmen, against many Communists and non-Party people, against economic executives and military men, against scientists and cultural personalities were a result of deliberate falsification.

Many of the accusations were later, especially after the 20th Party Congress, withdrawn. Thousands of innocent victims were completely exonerated.

But the process of restoring justice was not carried through and was actually suspended in the middle of the sixties. Now, in line with a decision taken by the October 1987 Plenary Meeting of the Central Committee, we are having to return to this. The Political Bureau of the Central Committee has set up a commission for comprehensively examining new and already known facts and documents pertaining to these matters. Appropriate decisions will be taken on the basis of the commission's findings.

All this will also be reflected in a treatise on the history of the Communist Party of the Soviet Union, which will be prepared by a special commission of the Central Committee. This is something we have to do, the more so since there are still attempts to turn away from painful matters in our history, to hush them up, to make believe that nothing special happened. We cannot agree to this. This would be disregard for the historical truth, disrespect for the memory of those who were innocent victims of lawless and arbitrary actions. Another reason why we cannot agree to this is that a truthful analysis must help us to solve today's problems of democratisation, legality, openness, overcoming bureaucracy, in short, the vital problems of perestroika. That is why here too we have to be quite clear, concise, and consistent.

An honest understanding of our enormous achievements as well as of past misfortunes, their full and correct political evaluation, will provide real moral guidelines for the future.

In drawing up a general balance-sheet of the period of the twenties and thirties after Lenin, we can say that we have covered a difficult road, replete with contradictions and complexities, but a truly heroic one. Neither gross errors, nor departures from the principles of socialism could divert our people, our country from the road it embarked upon by the choice it made in 1917. The momentum of the October Revolution was too great! The ideas of socialism that had gripped the masses were too strong! The people felt themselves involved in a great effort and began enjoying the fruits of their work. Their patriotism acquired a new, socialist meaning.

And all this was brought out forcefully in the grim trials of the Great Patriotic War of 1941-1945.

In the West there is now much talk about the situation on the eve of the war. Truths are being laced with half-truths. This is being done especially zealously by those who are displeased with the results of World War II—its political, territorial, and social results, by those who are bent on changing these results. That is why they are eager to present the historical truth upside down, to confuse the cause-and-effect relationships, and to falsify the chronology of events. In this context they are resorting to any lies in order to saddle the Soviet Union with the blame for World War II, the road to which was allegedly cleared by the Ribbentrop-Molotov non-aggression pact. This matter deserves greater consideration.

Actually, it was by no means on September 1, 1939, that World War II became a tragic reality. Japan's seizure of Northeast China (the "Manchurian incident" of 1931-1932), Italy's attack on Ethiopia (in 1935) and on Albania (in the spring of 1939), the German-Italian intervention against republican Spain (1936-1939), and Japan's armed invasion of North and then Central China (in the summer of 1937)—these were the initial conflagrations of World War II.

It is a different matter that in those days the West still pretended that this did not concern it or did not concern it enough to come to the defence of the victims of aggression. Hatred of socialism, long-term designs, and class selfishness prevented a sober assessment of the real dangers. Moreover, fascism was persistently being offered the mission of a strike force in an anti-communist crusade. Following Ethiopia and China, Austria and Czechoslovakia were flung into the furnace of "appeasement", the sword hung over Poland, over all the Baltic and Danube states, and propaganda was being conducted openly in favour of turning the Ukraine into a wheatfield and livestock farm of the "Third Reich". Ultimately, the main thrusts of aggression were being channelled against the Soviet Union, and since the scheming to divide up our country had begun long before the war, it is not hard to see how limited our options were.

It is said that the decision taken by the Soviet Union in concluding a non-aggression pact with Germany was not the best one. This may be so, if in one's reasoning one is guided not by harsh reality, but by abstract conjectures torn out of their time frame. In these circumstances, too, the issue was roughly the same as it had been at the time of the Brest Peace: was our country to be or not to be independent, was socialism on Earth to be or not to be.

The USSR made great efforts to build up a system of collective security and to avert a global slaughter. But the Soviet initiatives met with no response among the Western politicians and political intriguers, who were coolly scheming how best to involve socialism in the flames of war and bring about its head-on collision with fascism.

Outcasts already by virtue of our socialist birth, we could under no circumstances be right from the imperialist point of view. As I said, the Western ruling circles, in an attempt to blot out their own sins, are trying to convince people that the Nazi attack on Poland and thereby the start of World War II was triggered by the Soviet-German non-aggression pact of August 23, 1939. As if there had been no Munich Agreement with Hitler signed by Britain and France back in 1938 with the active connivance of the USA, no Anschluss of Austria, no crucifixion of the Spanish Republic, no Nazi occupation of Czechoslovakia and Klaipeda, and no conclusion of non-aggression pacts with Germany by London and Paris in 1938. By the way, such a pact was also concluded by pre-war Poland. All this, as you see, fitted neatly into the structure of imperialist policy, was and is considered to be in the nature of things.

It is known from documents that the date of Germany's attack on Poland ("not later than September 1") was fixed as early as April 3, 1939, that is, long before the Soviet-German pact. In London, Paris, and Washington it was known in minute detail how the preparations for the Polish campaign were really proceeding, just as it was known that the only barrier capable of stopping the Hitlerites could be the conclusion of an Anglo-Franco-Soviet military alliance not later than August 1939. These plans were also known to the leadership of our country, and that was why it sought to convince Britain and France of the need for collective measures. It also urged the Polish Government of the time to cooperate in curbing aggression.

But the Western powers had different designs: to beckon the USSR with the promise of an alliance and thereby to prevent the conclusion of the non-aggression pact we had been offered, to deprive us of the chance to make better preparations for the inevitable attack by Hitler Germany on the USSR. Nor can we forget that in August 1939 the Soviet Union faced a very real threat of war on two fronts: in the west with Germany and in the east with Japan, which had started a costly conflict on the Khalkhin-Gol.

But life and death, scorning myths, went into their real orbits. A new chapter was beginning in contemporary history, a most grim and complex one. At that stage, however, we managed to stave off the collision with the enemy, an enemy who had left himself and his opponent but one choice: to triumph or to perish.

The aggression to which we were subjected was a merciless test of the viability of the socialist system, of the strength of the multinational Soviet state, of the patriotic spirit of Soviet men and women. We withstood this test by fire and sword, comrades!

We withstood it because for our people this war became a Great Patriotic War, for in a struggle with such an enemy as German fascism the issue was one of life or death, was one of being free or of being enslaved.

We withstood it because this became for us a war of the entire people. Everyone rallied to the defence of the country: young and old, men and women, all the nations and nationalities of our great country. The generation born of the October Revolution and brought up by the socialist system likewise entered their first battle. Unprecedented staunchness and heroism on the battlefield, a courageous struggle by the partisans and underground resistance behind the enemy lines, and tireless work in the rear almost round the clock... That's what the war was for us.

Soviet men and women fought and worked to defend their country, the socialist system, the ideas and cause of the October Revolution. When this calamity came to our common home, the Soviet people did not flinch, did not falter—either under the blows of the initial setbacks and defeats, or under the weight of the millions of deaths, the torment and the suffering. From the first day of the war they had implicit faith in the coming Victory. In their soldiers' greatcoats and workers' overalls they did everything that was at the limit and beyond the limit of human endurance to hasten that long-awaited day. And when, on the 1418th day of the war, Victory did come, the entire delivered world heaved a sigh of relief, paying tribute to the victorious, heroic, and hard-working Soviet people, to their gallant Army, which had fought its way over thousands of kilometres, each of which had cost many lives and no end of blood and sweat.

The Great Patriotic War brought out to the full the talent of outstanding military leaders who had emerged from the midst of the people—Georgi Zhukov, Konstantin Rokossovsky, Alexander Vasilevsky, Ivan Konev, and other distinguished marshals, generals, and officers—those who commanded fronts and armies, corps, divisions, and regiments, companies and platoons. A factor in the achievement of Victory was the tremendous political will, purposefulness and persistence, ability to organise and discipline people displayed in the war years by Joseph Stalin. But the brunt of the war was borne by the ordinary Soviet soldier—a great toiler of the people's own flesh and blood, valiant and devoted to his country. Every honour and eternal glory to him!

Millions of veterans of the Great Patriotic War are in our ranks today too, taking a vigorous part in our revolutionary perestroika, in the renewal of society. Our filial thanks to them!

The moving spirit behind all our efforts on the battlefield and at work was our Leninist Party. At the front, in the trenches Communists were the first to rise to the attack, their example inspiring others; in the rear they were the last to leave their workbenches, the fields and livestock farms. Soviet men and women, as never before, sensed that the Communist Party was their party and that the Communists were showing in practice what it meant to be the people's vanguard at a time when the flames of war were raging and when the issue was one of life or death.

It may be said with confidence: the years of the Great Patriotic War are one of the most glorious and heroic pages in the history of the Party, pages inscribed by the courage and valour, by the supreme dedication and self-sacrifice of millions of Communists. The war showed that the Soviet people, the Party, socialism, and the October Revolution are inseparable and that nothing on earth can shatter this unity.

Socialism did not just stand fast and did not simply achieve victory. It emerged from this most terrible and destructive of wars stronger morally and politically, having enhanced its authority and influence throughout the world.

When the war ended, our ill-wishers predicted an economic decline in our country and its dropping out of world politics for a long time; they considered that it would take us half a century, if not more, to cope with the aftermath of the war. But within an extremely short period of time the Soviet people had rebuilt the war-ravaged towns and villages, and raised from their ruins factories and mills, collective and state farms, schools and colleges, and cultural institutions.

And once again this was a manifestation of the great strength of the socialist state: the will of the Party motivated by an understanding of the supreme interests of the Land of the October Revolution; the staunchness and proletarian wisdom of the workers, who had shouldered the main burden of the peaceful transformation of the country's industrial might and of repairing the ravages of war; and the self-sacrifice, patience, and patriotism of the farmers, who gave up everything they had to feed the ruined country. It was also a manifestation of the friendship of the peoples, of their mutual assistance, of their readiness— working together as brothers—to help those who had suffered particularly, to promote the recovery of those areas of our common Motherland that had been steamrollered especially mercilessly by the war.

It was the heroism of everyday work in those difficult post-war years that was the source of our achievements, of the economic, scientific and technical progress, of the harnessing of atomic energy, of the launching of the first spaceships, and of the growth of the people's economic and cultural standards.

But during this very same time—a time of new exploits by the people in the name of socialism—a contradiction between what our society had become and the old methods of leadership was making itself felt ever more appreciably. Abuses of power and violations of socialist legality continued. The "Leningrad case" and the "doctors' case" were fabricated. In short, there was a deficit of genuine respect for the people. People were devotedly working, studying, seeking new knowledge, accepting difficulties and shortages, but sensing that alarm and hope were building up in society. And all this gripped the public's consciousness soon after Stalin's death.

In the middle of the fifties, especially after the 20th Congress of the Communist Party, a wind of change swept the country, the people's spirits rose, they took heart, became bolder and more confident. It required no small courage of the Party and its leadership headed by Nikita Khrushchev to criticise the personality cult and its consequences, and to reestablish socialist legality. The old stereotypes in domestic and foreign policy began to crumble. Attempts were made to break down the command-bureaucratic methods of administration established in the thirties and the forties, to make socialism more dynamic, to emphasise humanitarian ideals and values, and to revive the creative spirit of Leninism in theory and practice.

The desire to change the priorities of economic development, to bring into play incentives related to a personal interest in work results keynoted the decisions of the September 1953 and July 1955 Plenary Meetings of the Party Central Committee. More attention began to be devoted to the development of agriculture, housing, the light industry, the sphere of consumption, and to everything related to satisfying human needs.

In short, there were changes for the better—in Soviet society and in international relations. However, no small number of subjectivist errors were committed, and they handicapped socialism's advance to a new stage, moreover doing much to discredit progressive initiatives. The fact is that fundamentally new problems of domestic and foreign policies and of Party development were often being solved by voluntaristic methods, with the aid of the old political and economic mechanism. But the failures of the reforms undertaken in that period were mainly due to the fact that they were not backed up by a broad development of democratisation processes.

At the October 1964 Plenary Meeting of the Party Central Committee there was a change of the leadership of the Party and the country, and decisions were taken to overcome voluntaristic tendencies and distortions in domestic and foreign policies. The Party sought to achieve a certain stabilisation in policy, and to give it realistic features and thoroughness.

The March and September 1965 Plenary Meetings of the Party Central Committee formulated new approaches to economic management. An economic reform and big programmes for developing new areas and promoting the productive forces were worked out and began to be put into effect. In the first few years this changed the situation in the country for the better. The economic and scientific potential was increasing, the defence capacity was being strengthened, and the standard of living was rising. Many foreign policy moves enhanced the international prestige of our state. Strategic parity with the USA was achieved.

The country had at its disposal extensive resources for further accelerating its development. But to utilise these resources and put them to work, cardinal new changes were needed in society and, of course, the corresponding political will. There was a shortage of both. And even much of what had been decided remained on paper, was left suspended in midair. The pace of our development was substantially retarded.

At the April 1985 Plenary Meeting of its Central Committee and at its 27th Congress the Party frankly identified the causes of the situation that had arisen, laid bare the mechanism retarding our development, and gave it a fundamental assessment.

It was stated that in the latter years of the life and activities of Leonid Brezhnev the search for ways of further advancement had been largely hampered by an addiction to habitual formulas and schemes which did not reflect the new realities. The gap between word and deed had widened. Negative processes in the economy were gathering momentum and had, in effect, created a pre-crisis situation. Many aberrations had arisen in the social, spiritual and moral spheres, and they were distorting and deforming the principles of socialist justice, undermining the people's faith in it, and giving rise to social alienation and immorality in various forms. The growing discrepancy between the lofty principles of socialism and the everyday realities of life was becoming intolerable.

The healthy forces in the Party and in society as a whole were becoming more and more acutely aware of the pressing need to overcome negative phenomena, to reverse the course of events, to secure an acceleration of the country's socio-economic development, and to bring about a moral purification and renewal of socialism.

It was in response to this extremely acute social need that the April 1985 Plenary Meeting of the Central Committee put forward the concept and strategy of accelerating the country's socio-economic development, and the course aimed at a renewal of socialism. These were given more elaborate theoretical and political formulation in the decisions of the 27th Party Congress and subsequent plenary meetings of the Central Committee, and assumed their final shape in the general policy of a revolutionary reorganisation of all the aspects of socialist society's life.

The idea of perestroika rests upon our seventy-year history, on the sound foundation of the basically new social edifice erected in the Soviet Union; it combines continuity and innovation, the historical experience of Bolshevism and what socialism is today. It is up to us to continue and carry forward the cause of the pioneers of the Revolution and of socialism. And we are certain to achieve this by our work, by making creative use of the experience of the generations that blazed the October trail before us and for us!

Comrades, we are following a revolutionary road, and this road is not for the weak and faint-hearted; this is a road for the strong and the brave. And that is what the Soviet people have always been—in the years of the greatest social transformations, in the years of ordeals of war, and in the years of peaceful constructive work. It is the people who shape their history, their destiny—never simple, but inimitable and invaluable, just as human life itself is. And this is one hundred times more true when we speak about the history of socialism, about continuing the cause of the Great Revolution.

The working class was and still is the cementing force and vanguard of the people. Even at the dawn of the revolutionary movement it followed Lenin's admonition: "Fight for freedom, without **even for a minute** abandoning the idea of socialism, without ceasing to work for its realisation, to prepare the forces and the organisation for the achievement of socialism." It was the working class, in alliance with all the working people, that carried out the Great October Revolution, that built socialism, and safeguarded it in bitter clashes with the enemy. It endured, suffered, and withstood everything! Today, too, it stands in the vanguard of developing socialism, of the revolutionary perestroika. Glory to it and great honour!

Our Leninist Party emerged and developed as a militant and active vanguard of the working class. It was from the working class that it gained its mighty confidence, firmness, discipline, and tenacity in the struggle for the ideals of socialism, its profound and humane understanding of life. Now, too, as a party of all the people, it has retained these finest features of that militant and constructive class. Today, as well as at every stage of socialism's history!

It is the principal definitive message of our history that all these seventy years our people have lived and worked under the Party's leadership in the name of socialism, in the name of a better and more just life. This is the destiny of a creative, constructive people!

II. Socialism in Development and Perestroika

Comrades, we have been led to the conclusion about the necessity for perestroika by pressing needs brooking no delay. But the more deeply we examined our problems and probed their meaning, the clearer it became that perestroika also has a broader socio-political and historical context.

Perestroika implies not only eliminating the stagnation and conservatism of the preceding period and correcting the mistakes committed, but also overcoming historically limited, outdated features of social organisation and work methods. It implies imparting to socialism the most contemporary forms, corresponding to the conditions and needs of the scientific and technological revolution, and to the intellectual progress of Soviet society. This is a relatively lengthy process of the revolutionary renewal of society, a process that has its own logic and stages.

Lenin saw the historic mission of socialism in the need to prepare by many years of effort for the transition to communism. The leader of the Revolution spoke highly of the ability of Marx and Engels "to analyse the transitional forms with the utmost thoroughness in order to establish, in accordance with the concrete historical peculiarities of each particular case, **from what and to what** the given transitional form is passing". In short, our teachers warned us repeatedly that the path of building the new society is a long series of transitions.

We have every reason to view perestroika as a definite historical stage in the forward movement of our society. And in reply to Lenin's question "from what and to what" we are passing, it must be said quite definitely: we have to impart to socialism a new quality or, as they say, a second wind, and this requires a profound renewal of all aspects of society's life, both material and spiritual, and the development of the humanitarian character of our system to the fullest possible extent.

The purpose of perestroika is the full theoretical and practical reestablishment of Lenin's conception of socialism, in which indisputable priority belongs to the working man with his ideals and interests, to humanitarian values in the economy, in social and political relations, and in culture.

Our hope of achieving revolutionary purification and renewal requires tapping the enormous social potentialities of socialism by invigorating the individual, the human factor. As a result of perestroika socialism can and must make full use of its potentialities as a truly humanitarian system serving and elevating man. This is a society for people, for the flourishing of their creative work, wellbeing, health, physical and spiritual development, a society where man feels he is the full-fledged master and is indeed that.

Two key problems of the development of society determine the fate of perestroika. These are the democratisation of all social life and a radical economic reform.

Perestroika, continuing as it does what the October Revolution began, has moved the task of deepening and developing socialist democracy to the forefront. The democratisation of society is at the core of perestroika, and on its progress depends the success of perestroika itself and—one can say without exaggeration—the future of socialism in general. This is the surest guarantee of changes, both political and economic, ruling out any movement backward.

The changes taking place in the country today constitute what is probably the biggest step in developing socialist democracy since the October Revolution.

In reorganising our economic and political system, it is our duty to create, first of all, a dependable and flexible mechanism for the genuine involvement of all the people in deciding state and public matters. Secondly, people must be taught in practice to live in the conditions of deepening democracy, to extend and consolidate human rights, to instill a contemporary political culture among the masses. In other words, to teach and to learn from each other about democracy.

As we mark the 70th anniversary of our Revolution and ponder over the future, we have to take a closer look at how the process of the democratisation of society is proceeding and what stands in its way. The difficulties and contradictions arising are considerable and at times unexpected; there is no avoiding a conflict between the new and advanced and the old and outdated. There is some uncertainty and hesitancy.

In the early days following the October Revolution Lenin pointed out that the workers and peasants were still "timid", still not resolute enough, not yet accustomed to the idea that it was for them to take over all the levers of administration. "But the Revolution of October 1917 is strong, viable and invincible," he wrote, "because it **awakens** these qualities, breaks down the old impediments, removes the worn-out shackles, and leads the working people on to the road of the **independent** creation of a new life."

Today, too, we see how difficult people find it to adapt to the new situation, to the possibility and necessity of living and solving all problems democratically. Many are still "timid", act irresolutely, fear responsibility, and are still in the grip of obsolete rules and instructions. The task is to cultivate in people a taste for independence and responsibility in their approach to production and social matters of any scale, to develop self-government as government of the people, exercised by the people themselves and in the interests of the people.

The development of self-government will proceed above all through the Soviets, which must, in accordance with the Party's plans, completely live up to their role as the authorised and the decision-making bodies. Lately, the rights and possibilities of the Soviets at all levels have been substantially extended. This process will continue. Consequently the Soviets will gain in strength and Soviet democracy will be deepened.

We have begun improving the electoral system. The elections held in June this year convinced us that the new approach is correct and fruitful. They showed the people's increased political activity, their interest in getting their really best representatives elected to the Soviets, although this time too there were instances of formalism and unnecessary regimentation.

Perestroika and the development of democracy make it possible to fully use the energy, potentialities, and power of the trade unions, the Young Communist League, and other public organisations, including those that have arisen in recent years, such as the All-Union Council of Veterans of War and Labour, the women's councils, the Cultural Foundation of the USSR, and V. I. Lenin Soviet Children's Fund. It is important that their everyday activities be connected with the solution of vital problems and reflect the interests of broad sections of the people.

Much that is new and encouraging has appeared in the work collectives and in neighbourhood activity. Broad opportunities are opening up for lofty initiatives, for solving all pressing problems promptly and without red tape.

The new processes taking place in the country also call for new approaches to the problems of general, political and legal culture, and to, I would say, the use of socialist democracy. It is the deficiencies in these areas that are largely responsible for such evils as bureaucracy, power abuses, kowtowing, and the waste and irresponsibility. The proper use of socialist democracy rejects methods of commands or "pressure", organisational vagueness, and the substitution of empty talk for deeds. All these are alien to socialism. It is also beyond doubt that the broader and deeper democracy is, the more attention must be given to socialist legality and law and order, the more we need organisation and conscientious discipline.

Democracy must not be confined to the political sphere. It must permeate all spheres of human relations. We proceed from the premise that socialism is a society of growing diversity in people's opinions, relationships, and activities. Every person has his own social experience, his own level of knowledge and education, his own perception of what is occurring. Hence, the tremendous variety of views, convictions, and assessments, which, naturally, require careful consideration and comparison. We are for a diversity of public opinion, a richness of spiritual life. We need not fear openly raising and solving difficult problems of social development, openly criticising and arguing. It is under such conditions that the truth is born and that correct decisions take shape. Socialist democracy must fully serve socialism, the interests of the working people.

Comrades, a sound basis for accelerated comprehensive forward movement can be created only through radical changes in the economy. Moreover, perestroika itself can gather full strength only when it produces profound changes in the national economy. And that in turn involves deep changes in the economic mechanism, in the entire system of economic management.

The purpose of the radical economic reform now under way in the country is to assure, over the next two or three years, a transition from a predominantly centralised command system of management to a democratic system based mainly on economic methods and on an optimal combination of centralism and self-management. This implies a radical expansion of the independence of enterprises and associations, their transition to the principles of self-accounting and self-financing, and the endowing of work collectives with all the powers necessary for this.

The economic reform is no longer just plans and intentions, still less abstract theoretical discourses. It is becoming a part of life. Today a considerable number of enterprises and associations in industry, construction, transport, and agriculture are working on the principles of self-financing and self-supporting. From the beginning of next year enterprises producing 60 per cent of our industrial output will be operating on this basis. The Law on the State Enterprise (Association) will have become effective.

All this is already having an effect on practical economic activity. Work collectives are showing a growing interest in the financial and economic results of their performance. They are beginning to keep track of inputs and outputs in a serious way, to save in things big and small, and to find the most effective ways of dealing with problems as they arise. Today we must once again firmly say: the Party will not tolerate any departure from the adopted principles of the economic reform implementation. All the scheduled changes must and will be carried out in full.

The economic reform and perestroika as a whole forcefully bring the individual to the forefront. Social justice requires that we give more attention to the specific abilities of each person, and reward morally and materially those who work better and more, those who set others a good example.

True talents and outstanding personalities are society's invaluable assets; they must be recognised, and all the necessary conditions must be created for their work and life. We want the dignity, knowledge, work, and ability of everyone to be respected everywhere. So that an honest, hard-working, creative person will know that his work will be properly appreciated, that he will always be given the chance to prove that he is right and will find support, while an idler, a moneygrubber, a bureaucrat, and a boor will be rebuffed and unmasked. The favourable changes that are taking place in our country—and they are receiving extensive coverage in the mass media—have the vigorous support of the people.

A sloppy attitude towards work is today particularly intolerable. The person who is armed with up-to-date knowledge and machinery produces more and more, and his work becomes increasingly dependent on the activities of the thousands of other participants in social production. In these circumstances the negligence of even a single worker, engineer, or scientist can have extremely grave consequences and is fraught with enormous losses for society.

I would like to emphasise the growing importance of intellectual work, of the interaction of science, technology, and society, of the humanitarian, moral and ethical aspects of science, and scientific and technical progress. We want that all the achievements of science and technology to be put at the service of man, and that they do not upset the environmental balance. We are drawing harsh lessons from such a tragic event as the Chernobyl nuclear power plant accident. We advocate an end to the use of science for military purposes. Today, engineers, scientists, physicians, educators, writers and those working in the arts must enhance their sense of social responsibility, their professional competence and make their creative achievements more worthwhile.

In restoring the principle of material incentives to its rightful place and in paying more attention to the collective forms of these incentives, we should not allow an underrating of socio-cultural, moral or psychological incentives. They are of exceptional importance for the normal development of the relations of collectivism and comradeship and the socialist way of life and for the firm establishment of our Soviet values in the thoughts and actions of our people.

Comrades, we have every right to say that the nationalities question has been solved in our country. The revolution paved the way for the equality of our nations not only in legal but also in socio-economic terms, having done a great deal to level up the economic, social and cultural development of all our republics, regions and peoples. One of the greatest gains of the October Revolution is the friendship of the Soviet peoples. It is, indeed, a unique phenomenon in world history. And for us, it is one of the chief buttresses of the strength and stability of the Soviet state.

Today, as we honour the outstanding achievements of the Leninist nationalities policy, the peoples of our country express their profound respect and gratitude to the great Russian people for its selflessness, its genuine internationalism and invaluable contribution to the creation, development and consolidation of the socialist Union of free and equal republics, to the economic, social, and cultural progress of all the peoples of the Soviet Union.

So, comrades, let us cherish our great common asset—the friendship of the peoples of the USSR. And let us, therefore, never forget that we are living in a multinational state, where all social, economic, cultural, and juridical decisions inevitably have a direct and immediate bearing on the nationalities question. Let us act as Lenin would, and build up the potential of every nation, everyone of the Soviet peoples, to the maximum.

National relations in our country are a vital issue in our life. We must be extremely considerate and tactful in all things that concern the national interests and national sentiments of people; we must ensure the most active participation of members of all nations and nationalities in fulfilling the diverse tasks of our multinational society. We intend to make a more indepth analysis and to discuss these issues in the nearest future with an eye to what perestroika, democratisation and the new stage in its development are introducing in the life of the country.

The friendship and cooperation of the peoples of the USSR are sacred to us. This has always been the case and will continue to be so. It is consonant with the spirit of Leninism, with the traditions of the October Revolution and with the vital interests of all nations and nationalities in our country.

Comrades, Soviet society's passage to a radically new quality, its breakthrough into the future is only possible along a broad front, which includes the intellectual sphere of socialist society—science and education, literature and art—and all the social and moral values of the Soviet people. Spiritual culture not only makes society's life more beautiful, it also performs functions essential to its existence and embodies its intellectual and cultural potential. It could be described as an agent strengthening the social fabric, as a catalyst of its dynamic development.

We should keep raising the prestige of socialist culture. Scholars, scientists, inventors, writers, journalists, artists, actors and teachers—all those who work in various spheres of culture and education—must be advocates of perestroika. The Party counts on our intelligentsia's vigorous civic and social involvement.

The Soviet people are now an enlightened people, something the great educators of the past could only dream about. But here, too, we cannot afford to be complacent. Our accomplishments should not allow us to close our eyes to the enormous scope and seriousness of the tasks we must tackle today. We see that the educational system has in many respects fallen short of today's requirements. The quality of education in schools, colleges and universities and of the training of workers and specialists does not fully meet the needs of the day.

We must surge ahead and bring about radical changes in this sphere too. That is the way the Party approaches the reform of secondary education and vocational training, the reorganisation in higher education. The CPSU Central Committee has decided to examine topical issues of education at one of its plenary meetings.

Such, comrades, are the strategic tasks we are to accomplish in the course of revolutionary perestroika covering all aspects of the life of socialist society.

Thirty months have elapsed since the April Plenary Meeting of the CPSU Central Committee. What are our achievements? What stage have we reached? I believe that raising these questions is both pertinent and essential at this jubilee session.

The general conclusion made on this score at the plenary meeting the CPSU Central Committee has just held is that we are at a turning point. By and large, we have passed through the first stage of our perestroika effort. A concept of perestroika has been worked out on the basis of an indepth analysis of the situation and of the outlook for the country's development. A fresh political, moral and psychological atmosphere has been created in our country. The Party has succeeded in making people more concerned about public affairs, in promoting their initiative, in making them more exacting, more critical and self-critical, in enhancing glasnost, and in paving the way for tangible changes in people's thinking and attitudes.

Support for perestroika and the demand that it make steady progress are the main features of the position taken by a majority of the Soviet people at the current stage. Industrial workers, collective farmers and the intelligentsia show understanding of the need to enhance discipline, efficiency and the quality of labour. A vigorous search for new forms of labour organisation and remuneration is under way at factories, construction sites, collective and state farms, and research establishments. People are making greater demands on themselves, on executives and experts, and they are combating mismanagement and irresponsibility. We greatly appreciate this civic stand of our people, and see it as an obvious and weighty expression of support for the course towards perestroika taken by the Party.

There is reason to speak of certain positive shifts that have occurred on the practical plane, first and foremost in the socio-economic sphere. Output growth rates have increased. Changes of a qualitative nature are in the offing in the economy, major scientific and technological programmes are under way, and our engineering industry is being modernised. The development of agriculture, particularly of animal husbandry, is showing increased stability.

You all know, comrades, how unfavourable the weather was in most regions of our country this year.

Nevertheless, we succeeded in harvesting more than 210 million tons of grain. This was the result of strenuous efforts by the people and by the Party which encouraged them to work in a new way.

The improvements that have begun in the economy have made it possible to initiate important measures in the social sphere. The scale of housing construction has increased noticeably, and the service sector is expanding. The incomes of working people are growing. The salaries of teachers and medical personnel have been raised. Major programmes are being implemented in education and health care.

Still, all that is only a beginning. Today we can say that we are entering a new stage of perestroika, the stage at which all our policies, all our decisions are taking the shape of practical action, being translated into reality. This calls for a great effort on the part of all our people—the working class, the farmers, the intelligentsia, and all our cadres. From now on, our ideas, plans, attitudes and methods of work will have to pass the test of practical application.

One can now feel a growing pressure in everything. But that is the vibrant pressure of creative, vigorous effort, of political and intellectual activity. There is a mobilising quality to this pressure, comrades, and it makes you feel good.

I would like to stress that viewed from this angle, the next two or perhaps three years will be particularly complicated, decisive and, in a sense, critical. The principal reason is that we will have to simultaneously tackle large-scale tasks in the economy, in the social sphere, in the reorganisation of government and public administration, in ideology and in culture.

In the economic sphere, we must effect far-reaching structural changes, achieve a breakthrough in accelerating scientific and technological progress, largely reorganise the economic mechanism, and thus take a decisive step in switching the economy to the track of intensive development.

The difficulty of the forthcoming period also lies in the fact that the transformations will come to affect the interests of ever greater masses of people, social groups and strata, and of all cadres. We are confident that widespread support of perestroika by the people and a profound understanding of the need for the changes, for the vigorous and unflagging pursuit of perestroika despite the difficulties arising in its course will continue to shape the situation in our country.

But it would be a mistake to take no notice of a certain increase in the resistance of the conservative forces that see perestroika simply as a threat to their selfish interests and objectives. This resistance can be felt not only at management level but also in work collectives. Nor can one really doubt that the conservative forces will seize upon any difficulty in a bid to discredit perestroika and provoke dissatisfaction among the working people. Even now there are those who prefer to keep count of the slipups instead of getting down to combating shortcomings and looking for new solutions. Naturally, these people never say that they oppose perestroika. Rather, they would have us believe that they are fighting against its negative side-effects, that they are guardians of the ideological principles that supposedly might be eroded by the increasing activity of the masses.

But, comrades, isn't it time to stop trying to scare us with all sorts of slipups? Of course negative side-effects are inevitable in any undertaking, particularly if it is novel. But the consequences of marking time, of stagnation and indifference have a much greater impact and cost a lot more than the side-effects that arise temporarily in the course of a creative effort to establish new forms of society's life.

We should learn to spot, expose and neutralise the manoeuvres of the opponents of perestroika—those who act to impede our advance and trip us up, who gloat over our difficulties and setbacks, who try to drag us back into the past. Nor should we succumb to the pressure of the overly zealous and impatient—those who refuse to accept the objective logic of perestroika, who voice their disappointment with what they regard as a slow rate of change, who claim that this change does not yield the necessary results fast enough. It should be clear that one cannot leap over essential stages and try to accomplish everything at one go.

Perestroika carries on the revolutionary cause, and today it is absolutely essential to master the skill of exercising revolutionary self-restraint. This self-restraint does not mean that we should sit back or drift with the current. It implies an ability to assess the situation realistically, not to back down before difficulties, not to panic, not to lose one's head over either success or failure—an ability to work strenuously and purposefully every day and every hour, to find and apply in everything the best possible solutions dictated by life itself.

Hence the need for confident, unswerving and purposeful efforts to implement what we have mapped out, to attain the objectives and accomplish the tasks that have been set. Our approach should consist in identifying and analysing contradictions, grasping their nature and, on this basis, devising a system of political, economic, social, organisational and ideological measures. That is the only approach.

Comrades, the success of perestroika depends above all on the energy and commitment of the Party and of every Communist, on the force of their example. At this juncture of historic responsibility, at this time of socio-economic transformations, the Communist Party has boldly launched a resolute struggle for society's renewal and taken on the most difficult part of the task. We can say with confidence that the great cause of the October Revolution, the cause of revolutionary perestroika, is in firm hands. The Communists will discharge their duty with a high sense of responsibility before our people and our age.

The priority task today is to radically improve the activities of Party organisations, of Party bodies and cadres. We must bring about a breakthrough in the work of every Party organisation; every Party committee and every Communist should step up their efforts. Things have started moving and decisively at that wherever this has been done, wherever Party leaders and Communists have aroused the initiative and enterprise of the masses, wherever they have boldly taken the path of democratisation and glasnost, of cost-effective management and the collective contract, wherever the door has been opened to new forms of labour organisation and incentives, of meeting human needs. But we can see that some cities, districts and regions, and even some republics have not yet got down to perestroika in earnest. That is a direct result of political and organisational inertia and lack of initiative displayed by Party committees and their leaders. This also should be seen. This is also our realities.

A turn for the better is a special responsibility that now rests with the primary Party organisations. They are in fact at the heart of perestroika. It is the initiative of the primary Party organisations on which the progress of the transformations, the skill in mobilising and inspiring people, and the ability to achieve tangible improvements depend above all. To sum up, comrades, perestroika will not succeed without a drastic invigoration of the activities of all Party organisations. And so we must have a more businesslike and a more democratic attitude, we must improve organisation and tighten discipline. Then we will be able to put perestroika into high gear and impart a new impetus to socialism in its development.

III. The October Revolution and Today's World

Comrades, without the Great Revolution in Russia, the world would not be what it is today. Before that turning point in world history, the "right" of the strong and the rich, as well as annexationist wars, were a customary and standard feature of international relations. The Soviet government, which promulgated the famous Decree on Peace as its first legal act, rose against this state of affairs and introduced into international practice something that used to be excluded from "big politics"—the people's common sense and the interests of the working masses.

During the few years when Lenin directed Soviet foreign policy, he not only worked out its underlying principles but also showed how they should be applied in a most unusual and abruptly changing situation. Indeed, contrary to initial expectations, the rupture of the "weakest link" in the chain of the capitalist system was not the "last, decisive battle" but the beginning of a long and complex process.

It was a major achievement of the founder of the Soviet state that he discerned in time the actual prospects the victory in the Civil War opened before the new Russia. He realized that the country had secured not merely a "breathing-space" but something much more important—"a new period, in which we have won the right to our fundamental international existence in the network of capitalist states". In a resolute step, Lenin suggested a policy of learning and mastering the art of long-term "existence side by side" with them. Countering leftist extremism, he argued that it was possible for countries with different social systems to coexist peacefully.

It took only 18 to 24 months in the wake of the Civil War to end the international political isolation of the state of workers and peasants. Treaties were concluded with neighbouring countries and then, at Rapallo, with Germany. Britain, France, Italy, Sweden and other capitalist countries extended diplomatic recognition to the Soviet Republic. The first steps were taken to build equitable relations with Oriental countries—China, Turkey, Iran and Afghanistan.

These were not simply the first victories of Lenin's foreign policy and diplomacy. They were a breakthrough into a fundamentally new quality of international affairs. The main trend of our foreign policy was established. We have every right to describe it as a Leninist policy of peace, mutually beneficial international cooperation and friendship among nations.

Naturally, not all our subsequent foreign policy efforts were successful. We have had our share of setbacks. We did not make full use of all the opportunities that opened before us both before and after World War II. We failed to translate the enormous moral prestige with which the Soviet Union emerged from the war into effective efforts to consolidate the peaceloving, democratic forces and to stop those who orchestrated the Cold War. We did not always respond adequately to imperialist provocations.

It is true that some things could have been tackled better and that we could have been more efficient. Nevertheless, we can say on this memorable occasion that the fundamental line of our policy has remained in concert with the basic course worked out and charted by Lenin—consonant with the very nature of socialism, with its principled commitment to peace.

This was overwhelmingly instrumental in averting the outbreak of a nuclear war and in preventing imperialism from winning the Cold War. Together with our allies, we defeated the imperialist strategy of "rolling back socialism". Imperialism had to curb its claims to world domination. The results of our peace-loving policy were what we could draw on at the new stage to devise fresh approaches in the spirit of the new thinking.

Naturally, there have been changes in the Lenin's concept of peaceful coexistence. At first it was needed above all to create a modicum of external conditions for the construction of a new society in the country of the socialist revolution. Continuing the class-based policy of the victorious proletariat, peaceful coexistence subsequently became a condition for the survival of the entire human race, especially in the nuclear age.

The April 1985 Plenary Meeting of the CPSU Central Committee was a landmark in the development of Leninist thought along this line too. The new concept of foreign policy was presented in detail at the 27th Congress. As you know, this concept proceeds from the idea that for all the profound contradictions of the contemporary world, for all the radical differences among the countries that comprise it, it is interrelated, interdependent and integral.

The reasons for this include the internationalisation of the world's economic ties, the comprehensive scope of the scientific and technological revolution, the essentially novel role played by the mass media, the state of the Earth's resources, the common environmental danger, and the crying social problems of the developing world which affect us all. The main reason, however, is the problem of human survival. This problem is now with us because the development of nuclear weapons and the threatening prospect of their use have called into question the very existence of the human race.

That was how Lenin's idea about the priority of the interests of social development acquired a new meaning and a new importance.

Since the April Plenary Meeting we have made our vision of progress towards a safe world and durable peace sufficiently clear to everyone. Our intentions and our will are recorded in the decisions taken by the highest political forum of the Party—the 27th Congress—as well as in the new edition of the CPSU Programme, in the programme for nuclear disarmament set forth in the Statement of January 15, 1986, in the Delhi Declaration, in other documents, and in official statements by the Soviet Union's leaders.

Acting jointly with the other countries of the socialist community, we have submitted several important initiatives to the United Nations, including a project for devising a comprehensive system of international peace and security. The Warsaw Treaty states have addressed NATO and all European countries with a proposal on reducing armed forces and armaments to a level of reasonable sufficiency. We have suggested comparing the two alliances' military doctrines in order to make them exclusively defensive. We have put forward a concrete plan for the prohibition and elimination of chemical weapons and are working vigorously in this direction. We have advanced proposals on devising effective methods for the verification of arms reductions, including on-site inspection.

We have come out resolutely for strengthening the prestige of the United Nations, for the full and effective use of the powers conferred upon it and its agencies by the international community. We are doing our best to enable the United Nations, a universal mechanism, to competently discuss and ensure a collective search for a balance of interests of all countries, and to discharge its peacemaking functions effectively.

The most important thing is that our concept and our firm dedication to peace are reflected in practical action, in all our international moves, and in the very style of our foreign policy and diplomacy which are permeated with a commitment to dialogue—a frank and honest dialogue conducted with due regard for mutual concerns and for the advances of world science, without attempting to outmanoeuvre or deceive anyone. And so, now that more than two years have elapsed, we can say with confidence that the new political thinking is not merely another declaration or appeal but a philosophy of action and, if you will, a philosophy of a way of life. In its development, it is keeping pace with objective processes under way in our world, and it is in fact already working.

The October 1986 meeting in Reykjavik ranks among the events which have occurred since the new stage in international affairs began, which deserve to be mentioned on this occasion and which will go down in history. The Reykjavik meeting gave a practical boost to the new thinking, enabled it to gain ground in diverse social and political quarters, and made international political contacts more fruitful.

The new thinking with its regard for universal human values and emphasis on common sense and openness, is forging ahead on the international scene, destroying the stereotypes of anti-Sovietism and dispelling distrust of our initiatives and actions.

It is true that, gauged against the scope of the tasks mankind will have to tackle to ensure its survival, very little has so far been accomplished. But a beginning has been made, and the first signs of change are in evidence. This is borne out, among other things, by the understanding we have reached with the United States on concluding in the near future an agreement on medium- and shorter-range missiles.

The conclusion of this agreement is very important in itself: it will, for the first time, eliminate a whole class of nuclear weapons, be the first tangible step along the path of scrapping nuclear arsenals, and will show that it is in fact possible to advance in this direction without prejudice to anyone's interests.

That is obviously a major success of the new way of thinking, a result of our readiness to search for mutually acceptable solutions while strictly safeguarding the principle of equal security.

However, the question concerning this agreement was largely settled back in Reykjavik, at my second meeting with the US President.

In this critical period the world expects the third and fourth Soviet-US summits to produce more than merely an official acknowledgement of the decisions agreed upon a year ago, and more than merely a continuation of the discussion. The growing danger that weapons may be perfected to a point where they will become uncontrollable is urging us to waste no time.

That is why we will work unremittingly at these meetings for a palpable breakthrough, for concrete results in reducing strategic offensive armaments and barring weapons from outer space—the key to removing the nuclear threat.

What, then, are the reasons for our optimism, for regarding comprehensive security really attainable? This deserves to be discussed here in detail.

At this new turning point in world history as we are celebrating the 70th anniversary of our Revolution which could not have won without theoretical preparation, we are examining the theoretical aspects of the prospects of advancement toward durable peace. The new way of thinking has helped us to generally prove that a comprehensive system of international security in the context of disarmament is needed and possible. Now we must prove that the attainment of this goal is necessary and feasible. We must identify the laws governing the interaction of the forces which, through rivalry, contradictions and conflicting interests, can produce the desired effect. In this connection we should begin by posing some tough questions—of course, tackling them from Leninist positions and using Leninist methodology.

The first question concerns the nature of imperialism. We know that it is the major source of the war threat. It goes without saying that external factors cannot change the nature of a social system. But, given the current stage of the world's development and the new level of its interdependence and integration, is it possible to influence that nature and block its more dangerous manifestations? In other words, can one be sure that the laws operating in the integral world, in which universal human values have top priority, will restrict the scope of the destructive effects produced by the operation of the egocentric laws which benefit only the ruling classes and are basic to the capitalist system?

The second question is connected with the first one: can capitalism get rid of militarism and function and develop in the economic sphere without it? Is it not a delusion on our part to invite the West to draw up and compare conversion programmes for switching economies over to civilian production?

The third question: can the capitalist system do without neocolonialism which is currently one of the factors essential to its survival? In other words, can this system function without the inequitable trade with the Third World which is fraught with unforeseeable consequences?

Another related question: how realistic is our hope that the awareness of the terrible threat the world is facing—and we know that this awareness is making its way even into the higher echelons of the Western ruling elite—will become a part of practical policies? After all, however forceful the arguments of common sense, however well-developed the sense of responsibility, however powerful the instinct of self-preservation, there are still things which must not be underrated and which are determined by economic and, consequently, class-based interest.

In other words, the question is whether capitalism can adapt itself to the conditions of a nuclear-weapon-free world, to the conditions of a new and equitable economic order, to the conditions in which the intellectual and moral values of the two world systems will be compared honestly. These are far from idle questions. The course history will take in the next decades will depend on the way they are answered.

But even posing these questions is enough to grasp the gravity of the task that lies ahead. We will see them answered in due time. Meanwhile, the viability of the programme for a nuclear-free and safe world will not only depend on its flawless scientific substantiation but will also be tested by the course of events—something that is influenced by a wide variety of factors, many of them new.

It is in fact already being tested. Here, too, we are loyal to the Leninist tradition, to the very essence of Leninism—an organic blend of theory and practice, an approach to theory as a tool of practice and to practice as a mechanism verifying the viability of theory. This is how we are acting, introducing a new way of thinking into our foreign policy activities, adjusting it and defining it more clearly using the political experience gained in practice.

To sum up, what are we counting on when we know that a safe world will have to be built jointly with capitalist countries?

The postwar period has witnessed an indepth modification of the contradictions that used to determine the principal trends in the world's economy and politics. I refer above all to the trends that inevitably led to wars, to world wars between capitalist countries themselves.

Today the situation is different. It is not only the lessons of the past war but also the fear of sapping its own strength in the face of socialism, by now a world system, that have prevented capitalism from allowing its internal contradictions to go to extremes. These contradictions began to evolve into a technological race and were dampened with the help of neocolonialism. A kind of new "peaceful" repartitioning of the world was started, in line with the rule Lenin identified—"according to capital", the bigger share going to whoever was strongest and wealthiest at the moment. Some countries began to "ease" tensions in their economies by rechannelling resources into the military-industrial complex on the pretext of a "Soviet threat". The changes occurring within the technological and organisational infrastructure of the capitalist economy also helped to clear up contradictions and to balance different interests.

But that is not all there is to it. Since an alliance

between a socialist country and capitalist states proved possible in the past, when the threat of fascism arose, does this not suggest a lesson for the present, for today's world which faces the threat of nuclear catastrophe and the need to ensure safe nuclear power production and overcome the danger to the environment? These are all perfectly real and acute problems. Grasping them is not enough: practical solutions must also be found.

The next point. Can a capitalist economy develop without militarisation? This brings to mind the "economic miracle" in Japan, West Germany and Italy—although it is true that when the "miracle" came to an end, they switched back to militarism again. But here one should examine the degree to which this switch was rooted in the essential laws governing the operation of contemporary monopoly capital and the role played by extraneous factors—the "contagious example" of the US military-industrial complex, the Cold War and its spirit, considerations of prestige, the need to have one's own "mailed fist" to be able to talk to one's competitors in a commonly understood language, and the desire to back one's economic invasion of the Third World with power politics. Whatever the actual reasons, there was a period when the modern capitalist economy developed rapidly in several countries whose military spending was minimal. The relevant historical experience is available.

This issue can also be considered from a different angle—the other way round. Ever since the war, the US economy has been oriented toward and dependent on militarism which at first seemed even to stimulate it. But then this senseless and socially useless squandering of resources led to an astronomical national debt and to other problems and maladies. In the final analysis it has turned out that supermilitarisation increasingly aggravates the domestic situation and upsets the economies of other countries. The recent panic on the New York Stock Exchange and on other stock exchanges around the world—a panic without precedent in almost 60 years—is a grave symptom and a grave warning.

The third point: the inequitable, exploitative relations with the developing countries. For all the fantastic innovations in the development of "alternative" (man-made) resources, developed capitalism has been and will be unable to do without these countries' natural resources. That is an objective fact.

The calls for severing the historically shaped world economic ties are dangerous and offer no solution. But the neocolonialist methods of using the resources of others, the arbitrary practices of the transnational corporations, the bondage of debt, debts that are nearing the trillion-dollar mark and obviously cannot be repaid, also lead to an impasse. All this gives rise to acute problems within the capitalist countries themselves too. The various speculations on this score are essentially aimed at making the Third World a kind of scapegoat and blaming it for the numerous difficulties—including the declining living standards—in the major capitalist countries.

Attempts are made time and again to "rally the nation together" on a chauvinistic basis, to lure the working people into a "partnership" in the exploitation of other countries, while making the masses accept the policy of new capitalist modernisation. However, none of these or similar stratagems can do away with the problem itself. They can only mitigate it temporarily. Inequitable trade remains a fact that will eventually culminate in an explosion. It appears that Western leaders are beginning to understand that this outcome is a distinct possibility, but so far they have been merely trying to resort to various palliatives.

Indeed, the novelty of the international economic and political processes of our time has not yet been fully grasped and assimilated. Yet, this will have to be done because the ongoing processes have the force of an objective law: there will either be a disaster or a joint quest for a new economic order which takes into account the interests of all on an equal basis. We see the way to establishing such an order in the implementation of the "disarmament-for-development" concept.

Thus, when looking for an answer to our third question, too, we see that the situation does not seem to defy resolution. In this area as well contradictions can be modified. But this necessitates understanding reality and mapping out practical actions in the spirit of a new thinking. And this, in turn, will facilitate the advance toward a more secure world. In a nutshell, here as well we are facing a historic choice dictated by the laws of our largely interconnected and integral world.

There is another important, even decisive, fact. Socialism is a component part of this world. Having begun its history 70 years ago and then grown into a world system, it has in fact determined the character of the 20th century. Today it is entering a new stage in its development, demonstrating, once again, its inherent potentialities.

Think, for instance, of the vast potential for peaceful coexistence inherent in just the Soviet Union's perestroika. By making it possible for us to attain the world level in all major economic indicators, perestroika will enable our vast and wealthy country to become involved in the world division of labour and resources in a way never known before. Its great scientific, technological and production potential will become a far more substantial component of world economic relations. This will decisively broaden and strengthen the material base of the all-embracing system of peace and international security. And that, by the way, is another highly important aspect of perestroika, the place it is assigned in contemporary civilisation.

The class struggle and other manifestations of social contradictions will influence the objective processes favouring peace.

The advanced forces of the working-class movement are looking for ways to enhance its political awareness. They have to carry on their activities in a highly complicated, new and changing situation. The issues involved in safeguarding the economic rights and interests of the masses, and indeed those related to the struggle for democracy, including democracy in production, have acquired a new meaning. For instance, workers are sometimes offered a "partnership", but it is a partnership under which the sanctum of business is inaccessible to them and free election of the managerial personnel is out of the question.

The Western world abounds in "theories" claiming that the working class is disappearing, that it has become completely absorbed by the "middle class", that it has changed socially, and so on and so forth. True, the changes undergone by the working class are substantial and far-reaching. But it is in vain that its class adversary is seeking consolation in this and trying to disorient and confuse the working-class movement. The working class, a numerically predominant force today within its new social boundaries, has the potential to play a decisive role, especially at abrupt turning points in history.

The motives for that may be different. One of the most probable ones is the insane militarisation of the economy. The transition to a new phase of the technological revolution on militarist grounds may serve as a powerful catalyst, especially as it paves the way to war, thus affecting all sections of the population and taking mass protests beyond the confines of economic demands. Therefore, here, too, the ruling class, the masters of monopoly capital, will have to make a choice. It is our belief, and it is confirmed by science, that at the present level of technology and organisation of production, the reconversion and demilitarisation of the economy are feasible. This would be tantamount to opting for peace.

The same concerns the consequences of the crisis in relations between the developed and the developing world. If things come to the verge of an explosion and it proves no longer possible to enjoy the benefits of exploiting the Third World, the question of the unacceptable and inadmissible character of a system unable to exist without this may acquire a political dimension and become very acute. In general, in this sense, too, capitalism is facing a limited choice—either to let things reach the breaking point or to heed the laws of the interconnected and integral world, one that calls for a balance of interests on an equal basis. The situation, as we see it, makes this not only necessary, but possible too. All the more so since forces in the Third World are acting along the same lines.

The decline of the national liberation movement is a common phrase. However, what is apparently happening is that one concept is being replaced by another and the novelty of the situation is being ignored. As far as the impulse for liberation is concerned, the one that was present at the stage of the struggle for political independence, it is certainly waning. And this is only natural. As for the impulse essential to the new, current stage of the Third World's development, it is only just beginning to be formed. One has to be aware of this and refrain from yielding to pessimism.

The factors that make up the impulse are varied and heterogeneous. Among them is a powerful economic process which sometimes takes on paradoxical forms. For instance, certain countries, while retaining some features of backwardness, are reaching the level of a great power in the world economy and politics. There is also an increase in political vigour in the process of the formation of nations and the strengthening of genuine nation-states, among which an important place is held by countries with revolutionary regimes. There is also the wrath bred by the dramatic polarisation of poverty and wealth, and the contrast between possibilities and realities.

An urge for national identity and independence makes itself increasingly felt in the organisations reflecting the processes of inter-state consolidation among the developing countries. To a greater or lesser extent this is characteristic of all the organisations, and their number is not small—the Organisation of African Unity, the League of Arab States, the ASEAN, the Organisation of American States, the Latin American Economic System, the South Pacific Forum, the South Asian Association for Regional Cooperation, the Organisation of the Islamic

Conference and, especially, the Non-Aligned Movement.

They represent a wide spectrum of conflicting interests, needs, aspirations, ideologies, claims, and prejudices typical of precisely this stage. Although they have already turned into a noticeable factor in world politics, none of them has yet fully revealed its potentialities. But their potentialities are colossal, and it is even hard to predict what they will yield in the next 50 years.

One thing is clear: this is a world of its own, seeking organisational forms for effective and equitable participation in solving problems common to the whole of humankind. It represents two and a half billion people. One can envision the gigantic strides it will make not only in exerting its influence on world politics, but also in playing an original role in shaping the world economy of the future.

For all their might, it is not the transnationals that will determine the Third World's development; it is more likely that they will be forced to adjust to the independent choice that has been or will be made by the peoples. The peoples and the organisations representing them are vitally interested in the new world economic order.

There is another important point to be made. In the last few decades, development within the capitalist world itself has given rise to new forms of social contradictions and movements. These include movements to remove the nuclear threat, protect the environment, eliminate racial discrimination, rule out policies dividing society into the privileged and the underprivileged, prevent the disaster threatening industrial areas that have fallen victim to present-day capitalist modernisation. These movements involve millions of people and are inspired and led by prominent figures in science and culture, people enjoying national and international prestige.

Social democratic, socialist and labour parties and mass organisations similar to or connected with them are continuously playing an important role in the political processes in a number of countries, and in some countries they are increasing their influence.

Thus, according to all economic, political and social indications everywhere in today's world the thesis Lenin regarded as one of the most profound in Marxism is being vindicated: as the soundness of a historical action increases, the masses involved in this action will grow in number as well. And this is always an unmistakable sign and the most powerful factor of social progress and, consequently, of peace.

Indeed, the grandeur and novelty of our time is determined by the peoples' increasingly obvious and open presence in the foreground of history. Their present positions are such that they must be heeded immediately rather than in the long run. The new truth thereby brought into sharp focus is that the constant need to make a choice is becoming increasingly characteristic of historical advancement on the threshold of the 21st century. And the right choice depends on the extent to which the interests and aspirations of millions, of hundreds of millions of people are heeded.

Hence the politicians' responsibility. For policy can only be effective if the novelty of the time is taken into account—today the human factor figures on the political plane not as a remote and more or less spontaneous side effect of the life, activity and intentions of the masses. It directly invades world affairs. Unless this is realised, in other words, unless a new thinking, one based on current realities and the peoples' will, is adopted, politics turn into an unpredictable improvisation posing a risk both to one's own country and to other nations. Such politics have no lasting support.

Such are the reasons for our optimistic view of the future, of the prospects of creating an all-embracing system of international security.

This is the logic behind our stand on defence issues, too. As long as there is a danger of war and as long as the drive for social revanche remains the core of Western strategies and militarist programmes, we shall continue to do everything necessary to maintain our defence capability at a level ruling out imperialism's military superiority over socialism.

Comrades, during these jubilee days, we duly commend the accomplishments of the world communist movement. The October Revolution, which has retained to this day its international momentum, is the source of the movement's viability. The world communist movement grows and develops upon the soil of each of the countries concerned, but there is something that the image of a Communist has in common, no matter what his nationality is, no matter what country he works in. It is loyalty to the idea of the best, communist society, loyalty to the working people—above all the working class, and the struggle for their vital interests, for peace and democracy.

I feel this anniversary is the right occasion to mention the Third, Communist International. The truth about it has yet to be restored in full, and its authentic and complete history has yet to be written. For all the drawbacks and errors in its activities and for all the bitterness the recollection of certain chapters in its history may evoke, the Communist International is part of our movement's great past. Born of the October Revolution, the movement has become not only a school of internationalism and revolutionary brotherhood. It has made internationalism an effective instrument furthering the interests of the working people and promoting the social progress of big and small nations. It has produced a whole galaxy of true knights of the 20th century, men of honour and responsibility, of lofty aspirations and unflinching courage, who took the sufferings of the millions of oppressed all over the world as their own, who heard their pleas and roused them to struggle.

Communists were the first to sound the alarm about the danger of fascism and the first to rise against it; they were also its first victims. They were the first—coming from all over the world—to engage in armed struggle against fascism in Spain. They were the first to raise the banner of Resistance in the name of the freedom and national dignity of their peoples. It was Communists, above all Soviet Communists, who made a decisive contribution to the crushing defeat of fascism in World War II.

And later, and today too, Communists have been fighting in the front ranks against reaction and obscurantism of every hue with the same irreconcilability and courage. They are people of legendary heroism and dedication. There are hundreds of thousands of them, organised and united by a single will, iron discipline, and commitment to their ideals.

The time of the Communist International, the Cominform, even the time of binding international conferences is over. But the world communist movement lives on. All parties are completely and irreversibly independent. We declared that as early as the 20th Congress. True, the old habits were not discarded at once. But today this has become an unalterable reality. In this sense, too, the 27th Congress of the CPSU was a final and irrevocable turning point. I think this has been actually proved by our relations with fraternal parties in the course of perestroika.

The world communist movement is at a turning point, just as is world progress itself and its motive forces. The communist parties are looking for their new place in the context of the profound changes unfolding as we are about to enter a new century. Their international movement is undergoing a renewal and is united by respect for the principles of confidence, equality, and sincere solidarity that have also been renewed. The movement is open to dialogue, cooperation, interaction and alliance with all other revolutionary, democratic and progressive forces.

The CPSU has no doubts about the future of the communist movement as one that offers an alternative to capitalism and involves the most valiant and consistent fighters for peace, for their countries' independence and progress, for friendship among all the peoples on Earth.

Comrades, the emergence of the world socialist system is the most important landmark in world history since the October Revolution. It is 40 years since socialism became the common destiny of many nations and a most important factor of contemporary civilisation.

Our Party and the Soviet people highly appreciate the opportunity to cooperate with our friends who, just like us, have also assumed responsibility on a state level for socialism and its advancement for several decades now. All the socialist states have accumulated a great deal of interesting and useful experience in solving social, economic and ideological tasks and in building a new life.

The socialist system, the quests and experience it has tested in practice are of importance to the whole of mankind. It has offered to the world its own answers to the main questions of human existence, and confirmed its humanitarian and collectivist values centered on the working man. The socialist system instills in him a sense of dignity, a feeling of being master of his own country; it gives him social protection and confidence in the future. It secures for him broad access to knowledge and culture, and creates conditions for putting the individual's abilities and gifts to good use.

We all take pride in what has been achieved by the peoples in socialist countries, especially because their achievements are an outcome of many years of fruitful cooperation, a result of the unprecedentedly broad, open and truly fraternal communication between these countries' citizens, Party and public organisations, production teams, professional unions, cultural establishments, a result of family and personal ties, and of the joint work and study of tens of thousands of people.

The heights reached enable us to have a clearer view of many things. Life has corrected our notions of the laws and rates of transition to socialism, our understanding of the role of socialism on the world scale. It would never occur to us to claim that all the progressive changes in the world are due to socialism alone. But the way mankind's vital problems have been posed, the way solutions to them are being sought prove that there is an inseparable link between world process and socialism as an international force. This link is especially evident in the struggle to avert nuclear catastrophe and in that balance of world forces which enables various peoples to more successfully uphold the socio-political choice they have made.

The accumulated experience ensures a better possibility of building relations between socialist countries on the following universally recognised principles:

— unconditional and full equality;

— the ruling party's responsibility for the state of affairs in the country; its patriotic service to the people;

— concern for the common cause of socialism;

— respect for one another; a serious attitude to what has been achieved and tested by one's friends; voluntary and diverse cooperation;

— a strict observance of the principles of peaceful coexistence by all. This is what the practice of socialist internationalism rests on.

Today the socialist world appears before us in all its national and social variety. This is good and useful. We have become convinced that unity does not mean identity and uniformity. We have also become convinced that there is no "model" of socialism to be emulated by everyone, nor can there be any.

The totality and quality of actual successes scored in restructuring society for the sake of the working people is the criterion of socialism's development at each stage and in each country.

We are aware of the damage that can be done to relations between socialist countries by a weakening of internationalist principles, by a departure from the principle of mutual benefit and mutual assistance, by a neglect of the common interests of socialism on the international scene.

We are pleased to state that of late our relations with all socialist states have become more dynamic and are improving. And cooperation in the framework of the Warsaw Treaty and CMEA certainly has become more fruitful and businesslike, which, however, does not set their member-countries in any essential way apart from other socialist countries.

The 27th Congress clearly defined the CPSU's position: that which ensures the combination of mutual interests with the interests of socialism as a whole is of decisive importance in politics and all other areas of our interaction with every socialist country. The strengthening of friendship and utmost development of cooperation with socialist countries is the top-priority goal of the Soviet Union's foreign policy. Welcoming today the delegations from socialist countries, we convey our greetings through them to the peoples of socialist countries.

Dear comrades,
Esteemed foreign guests,

In all our thoughts and deeds we have been inspired by the invigorating force of communist ideas. Inscribed on the banner of the Revolution, they inspired millions of people to struggle and labour, people who held these ideas sacred and regarded them as the purpose and meaning of their life.

The people's labour and struggle, their unabated perseverance in striving for their freely chosen goal, their joys and sufferings have become embodied in the reality of today's socialism advancing along the road of revolutionary perestroika. In this lies the force of the October Revolution, a revolution that continues.

For 70 years now the Soviet people have been led by their well-tried vanguard, the Leninist Party. The Party and revolution, the Party and the October Revolution are inseparable!

The victory of the socialist revolution would have been impossible without a party equipped with the Marxist-Leninist theory. Without the Party that learned to build a new society, there would be no socialism and there would not be our great country. Nor would we have a base for the present renewal of all aspects of society and for the country's accelerated socio-economic development. It is the imperative of the day that under the new conditions, too, the Party should take the lead in revolutionary renewal, enhancing, perseveringly and consistently, the effectiveness of its policy and promoting democratisation in all areas and at all levels of public life.

That the Party's role should grow is natural. But words and formal rituals have little to do with it. The Party's role is determined by the depth and honesty of analysis and assessment, by the well thought-out policies and resolute action, by the ability to correlate the particular and the general, the personal and the social, the present and the long-term. It is determined by the heightened responsibility of all Party organisations and of each Communist for the state of affairs in society.

Our Party has a membership of some 20 million, which equals one-tenth of the country's adult population. It is an enormous force. However, the potential of the Party's influence, the Party's impact on perestroika has not yet been fully brought into play. The preparation for and holding of the 19th All-Union Party Conference should give a powerful impetus to improving the complicated and intricate work along these lines.

Today, the fate of the great cause of the revolution, of the great Leninist cause is in our hands. We are again blazing the trail. And this imposes special responsibility on the Party, on all of us. To put it in Lenin's phrase, "The time of revolution is a time of action, of action from both above and below." This is the tradition that has been carried on by the party of a new type since its inception. This is also a demand made of the vanguard of Soviet society at the present stage in socialism's development which is both highly complicated and inspiringly novel.

Comrades, in 1917 humanity crossed the threshold and embarked on its true history. However, the past 70 years, the economic upheavals and social cataclysms that generated fascism and World War II, as well as the Cold War, the arms race, the threat of thermonuclear catastrophe and global crises have shown that the past still has a considerable part of humanity in its grip. And yet, we are justified in regarding the time we are living in, the juncture between the 20th and the 21st century, as unique in terms of the profound social changes and the global scope of the tasks that face the peoples of the world.

We can see today that humanity is not really doomed to always live the way it did before October 1917. Socialism has evolved into a powerful, growing and developing reality. It is the October Revolution and socialism that show humankind the road to the future and identify the new values of truly human relations:

— collectivism instead of egoism;

— freedom and equality instead of exploitation and oppression;

— genuine power of the people instead of the tyranny of the few;

— the growing role of reason and humanism instead of the spontaneous and cruel play of social forces;

— humankind's unity and peace instead of discord, strife and war.

The present generation, and not only that in our country, is responsible for the fate of civilisation and life on Earth. It is this generation that will determine, in the long run, whether the beginning of a new millennium in world history will be the latter's tragic epilogue or whether it will signal an inspiring prologue to the future.

Slightly more than thirteen years are left before the beginning of the 21st century. In the year 2017 the Soviet people and the whole of progressive humanity will mark the centenary of the Great October Revolution.

What is the world going to be like when it reaches our Revolution's centenary? What is socialism going to be like? What degree of maturity will have been attained by the world community of states and peoples? Let us not indulge in guessing. But let us remember that the foundations for the future are being laid today. It is our duty to preserve our inimitable civilisation and life on Earth, to help reason win over nuclear insanity, and to create all the necessary conditions for the free and all-round development of the individual and the whole of humanity.

We are aware that there is a possibility of infinite progress. We realise that it is not easy to ensure it. But this does not frighten us. On the contrary, this inspires us, giving a lofty and humane purpose to our life and injecting it with a profound meaning.

In October 1917 we parted with the old world, rejecting it once and for all. We are moving towards a new world, the world of communism. We shall never turn off that road!

> *(The report was heard with great attention and repeatedly punctuated with applause.)*